100 GREAT EFL QUIZZES, PUZZLES AND CHALLENGES

STIMULATING, PHOTOCOPIABLE, LANGUAGE ACTIVITIES FOR TEACHING ENGLISH TO CHILDREN AND YOUNG LEARNERS OF ESL AND EFL.

ADRIAN BOZON

CRAZY CHOPSTICK PUBLICATIONS

Contents

Foreword

Foreword

One of the key roles of a teacher is to ensure students are constantly consolidating previous learning as well as introducing new material. Lesson contents should be as stimulating as possible for the learners. The activities in this book are highly motivating for students of lower intermediate ability through to advance level learners. The various puzzles, quizzes and challenges are very effective at encouraging the students to work together and they nurture teamwork. Teachers can place students into pairs or small groups depending on class size and the ability of the children.

When choosing activities to use, it is important to consider the capabilities of the students very carefully and pitch the tasks at a level compatible with the students. Obviously, setting an activity that is far too difficult is going to be counterproductive. Likewise, while giving a relatively easy version of a quiz or puzzle as an introduction to the methods and technique involved can sometimes be useful for familiarizing the students, under normal circumstances a task that is not challenging enough for the students will not keep them focused for too long, not to mention that it will fail to advance their learning. More suitable are activities which challenge students but are possible to complete, or almost complete, after several minutes of thought and work, perhaps in collaboration with partners, sharing ideas within teams and/or with some limited hints or assistance from the teacher.

Whenever possible, be sure to go through the answers as a class at the end of an activity. As is the nature of quizzes, the students will kick themselves when they hear some of the answers they got wrong or could not think of within the time. However, some of the other questions may have answers containing vocabulary which is new or difficult for the students so clearly explain or illustrate unfamiliar words. Always look at the questions in detail before giving the activities to the students. If there are a couple of questions or so that are likely to prove difficult, consider what useful hints you could give the class before they start or prepare explanations, printouts, picture cards or illustrations such as having relevant internet images open on a classroom computer ready to show the students at the end.

After a lesson, make and keep notes of any questions the children struggled with, could not answer, misunderstood, or any other misconceptions they had, and use this information to guide you towards the best way of supporting other students when you try the same activity in the future with another class.

All of the activities in this book are photocopiable and ready for classroom use. They should be given as links to students' current or previous learning. Many cover particular topics or areas of grammar. Others, such as the quizzes, are of a more general nature and can be used at any suitable time. The ready to go nature of these tasks make them an invaluable resource for all teachers, old and new. I sincerely hope they will give your students a thorough workout and give them as much enjoyment as they have for mine.

I dedicate this book to Miyoung, Holly and Ellie, my lovely family.

Adrian Bozon

1

A-Z Quizzes

A-Z Quizzes

Students read the questions and try to answer as many questions as possible within a time limit. Use this game to practise the students' reading skills, vocabulary and potentially spelling too.

Choose a quiz appropriate for the level of the students* and put them into teams of about four or five students. Allow them approximately fifteen minutes to attempt all of the questions. The time can be adjusted slightly or an additional final one or two minutes can be given at the end of the time at the discretion of the teacher. Students read the questions and look at the letter. The starting letter of each answer must match the letter of the question. The answer to the X, Y) questions could start with either of those two letters. The teacher can help an individual team that is struggling to understand the meaning of a question but should only give broad hints for an answer to the whole class unless one team is clearly lagging a fair way behind the other teams.

When the time is over, ask teams to swap papers, go through the answers as a class and discuss any queries. Each correct answer scores one point. Wrong answers score nothing. In the case of right answers but with the wrong spelling, there is not necessarily a right or wrong way to proceed. These answers could be reduced to half points although it would be a lot more positive to focus on the use of accurate vocabulary to give the right answers in spite of spelling mistakes and still award a full point. One possibility would be to count the number of answers with spelling mistakes in the event of a tie to determine a winner. A perfect score is rare. Any score over twenty points is very good.

---

* If the class schedule allows it, the first time the students attempt this activity they could try one of the quizzes that are, perhaps, a level below their true standard e.g. upper intermediate level learners could try a lower intermediate level quiz or advanced learners could try an upper intermediate level quiz. This enables them to become used to the format, feel satisfaction of a good score the first time and prepares them for the challenge of the higher level quizzes a few days or weeks later.

A-Z Quiz One (Lower Intermediate)

A) Which fruit is small and usually red or green?

B) What do soccer players kick?

C) What animal is small and makes a miaow sound?

D) What do people often throw when they play a board game?

E) What food do we get from chickens?

F) What animal swims in water?

G) What is the opposite word to stop?

H) What five letter word do people say when they meet someone?

I) What food do people like to eat on a hot day?

J) What food moves?   Children like to eat it.

K) The female is a queen.   What is the male?

L) What does a heart often mean?

M) Which animal swings in trees?

N) What is four plus five?

O) Which animal has eight arms?

P) What has black and white keys and plays music?

Q) What word means no talking?

R) What is the weather when you use an umbrella?

S) What day comes after Friday?

T) What has leaves and grows outside?

U) What do people sometimes see in the sky?   Maybe there are aliens inside.

V) What looks like a small guitar and plays music?

W) Which fruit is green on the outside, red on the inside and often very big?

X, Y) What do doctors take to look at bones?

Z) Where do people often see animals?

A-Z Quiz Two (Lower Intermediate)

A) What helps people fly in the sky?

B) What do people eat in the morning?

C) What do children sit on at school?

D) What do all people do at the end of their life?

E) What are you studying now?

F) What is seven plus seven?

G) Which animal has a long neck?

H) If a boy is smiling, how is he feeling?

I) What do you do at an ice rink?

J) What do people sometimes put on bread or toast?

K) Which animal hops and lives in Australia?

L) Which body part do you put in jeans?

M) What shows the food and drinks in a restaurant?

N) What is the opposite word to yes?

O) Which colour can people eat?

P) What sport has a very small white ball and is played on a table?

Q) The male is a king. What is the female?

R) What has seven colours and is sometimes in the sky?

S) Where do children go every morning?

T) What do people watch in the living room?

U) What do people use when it is raining?

V) Where do many people put flowers?

W) Which season comes before spring?

X, Y) What colour is a banana?

Z) Which number is smaller than one?

A-Z Quiz Three (Lower Intermediate)

A) Which animal is long and looks like a crocodile?

B) What has two wheels and can be used to go to school?

C) What do people call December 25th?

D) What is the name of a tooth doctor?

E) What is nine plus nine?

F) What can you call a person with a big stomach?

G) What can you call your father's father?

H) How is the weather in the summer?

I) What is the opposite word to out?

J) What do people sometimes wear on their legs?   They are often blue.

K) What do soccer players do with a ball?

L) Where can you see lots of books?

M) What is in the sky at night?

N) What body part is on the face?

O) A baby is young.   What is a grandfather?

P) What do people give friends on their birthdays?

Q) What has many questions?   Sometimes you can find it in a book or on television.

R) Which animal has big, long ears?

S) What is a big boat called?

T) What do people do on the telephone?

U) What is the opposite word to down?

V) Which kind of foods do many children hate to eat?

W) What do many people wear on their arms to help them tell the time?

X, Y) The next day is tomorrow.   What is the day before today?

Z) What is the name of a black and white striped animal?

A-Z Quiz Four (Upper Intermediate)

A) When do most children go home from school?

B) Which sport has a field similar to a diamond shape?

C) Which bug changes into a butterfly?

D) What was a Tyrannosaurus Rex?

E) What word is the opposite of late?

F) Humans have hair.   What do animals and mammals have?

G) What are windows made from?

H) If a woman is beautiful, what is a man?

I) What do many people have before getting a job?

J) What do soccer players do before heading the ball?

K) What do many people use to open or unlock a door?

L) Which fruit is yellow and oval?

M) Who sometimes makes things disappear or pulls a bird or rabbit out of a hat?

N) What is the opposite word to always?

O) Shops close at night.   What do they do in the morning?

P) What are students studying when they go outside and play sports?

Q) What noise does a duck make?

R) What do cars travel on?

S) What is the ninth month of the year?

T) What is the name of the big bird people sometimes eat on special days?

U) The female is an aunt.   What is the male?

V) What is the name for an animal doctor?

W) What do we call it when two countries start fighting?

X, Y) What is the name of a toy that goes up and down.

Z) Who cares for the animals at a zoo?

A-Z Quiz Five (Upper Intermediate)

A) Which South American country plays soccer well?

B) Which snack do humans and dogs like?

C) How do babies move before they start walking?

D) What do people use to find the spelling and meanings of words?

E) Which big bird starts and finishes with the letter 'e'?

F) What do some people use in the house to give cool air on a hot day?

G) What is green and on the ground?   You see lots of it in parks and gardens.

H) What is the answer to one divided by two?

I) What kind of place is popular for a vacation?   You often have to use a boat to get there.

J) What do people sometimes tell to make other people laugh?

K) Which kind of toy do children like to fly in the sky?

L) What is a different word for a woman?

M) What do people watch in a cinema?

N) What word is used to describe a student or child who does lots of bad or silly things?

O) What kind of place usually has many computers, telephones, desks and workers?

P) Who flies an airplane?

Q) What is the answer of one divided by four?

R) What is like a computer and sometimes help humans?

S) What do we call it when the hot sun makes peoples' skin very red?

T) What sound does a clock often make?

U) Which horned animal is very popular in old stories?

V) Which special day is on February 14th?

W) What do people sometimes make before blowing out the candles on a birthday cake?

X, Y) Which healthy food is made from milk and can be eaten at any time of the day?

Z) What is a small area sometimes called?

A-Z Quiz Six (Upper Intermediate)

A) If you take some medicine or use some cream and then your skin starts to have problems, what problem might you have?

B) What is the past tense of buy?

C) What do many people sit on to make chairs more comfortable?

D) What do many people write in every day?   Often they do not show their friends or family.

E) What is the name of one of the biggest keys on a computer keyboard?

F) What is an area with a lot of trees called?

G) Sometimes people think they have seen dead people.   In pictures or children's stories they are usually white.   What do we call these images?

H) What special day is on October 31st?

I) Which country looks like a boot on a map?

J) Which kind of music often uses saxophones?

K) Where do people cook?

L) What falls off trees in the fall/autumn season?

M) What is the name of the red planet?

N) Which healthy food do squirrels like to eat?

O) What is the name of the tenth month of the year?

P) What is the name of the black and white bird that cannot fly but can swim well and usually lives in Antarctica?

Q) What is the opposite of slowly?

R) What do many people use to listen to music and news in their car?

S) What do people use when they wash their face or hands?

T) What is the name of one kind of very big spider?

U) What is the opposite of over?

V) What do we call it when people put an O or X next to a name and choose one person for an important job?

W) What can you call someone who often loses fights or cannot lift heavy things?

X, Y) What do most houses have outside?

Z) If you want to make the size of something bigger on a computer or video camera what can you do?

A-Z Quiz Seven (Upper Intermediate)

A) What do people write on envelopes?

B) What is the normal name for a bread shop?

C) What can we call people who go into shops to buy something?

D) What do people do with a spade?

E) What is a different word for a test?

F) What is the name of a large country in Western Europe?

G) In which school subject do students learn about Earth, land, countries and the environment?

H) What do we call something that is like a small mountain, which people walk up and down?

I) What do people use on a computer to find lots of information?

J) What has many small pieces and is a picture puzzle?

K) What do people sometimes do with their lips?

L) What is the opposite of early?

M) What animal is usually seen on a computer desk?

N) What is a short daytime sleep called?

O) Which bird is usually busy at night and sleeps during the day?

P) What do people usually put food on?

Q) What is the name of sand that people can sink into quickly?

R) What is on the top of a house?

S) What do people use when they wash their hair?

T) What do teams sometimes receive after winning a game or competition?   It often looks like a cup.

U) What do many school children wear?

V) What is the name of a popular ice cream flavour?

W) Which question word sounds like a letter?

X, Y) What do 365 days make?

Z) What do many coats and jackets have?

A-Z Quiz Eight (Advanced)

A) What do people call little green men that may live on other planets?

B) Which fruit is blue and very small?

C) What do we call an important cook in a restaurant?

D) Left, right and go straight are examples of what?

E) What is the name of the body part in the middle of each arm?

F) Which place has many workers and machines and makes lots of different things?

G) What is the English name for the very, very long wall in China?

H) What is the name of the small thing that golf players want to hit a ball into?

I) Which European country has green on the left side of its flag, white in the middle and red on the right side?

J) Which month is three months before April?

K) What is another name for children?

L) What is the name of a toy, which has lots of small coloured plastic bricks that children put together to make buildings, cars, robots and many other things?

M) How do we say 1,000,000 in English?

N) What do many people buy and read every day?

O) Which animal only has two letters in its name?

P) What is the name of a bird that can talk?

Q) What name is usually given to an English computer keyboard?

R) What do many people use to change the television channel ?

S) Which cold food has a different spelling but sounds the same as a day of the week?

T) What do students use to check their lesson schedule and other people use to check bus and train times?

U) What is the opposite word to lucky?

V) What are the blue lines called that you can see when you look at your skin?

W) What do some people wear on their head if they do not have much hair?

X, Y) What does a tired person do when opening his or her mouth?

Z) Which country borders South Africa?

A-Z Quiz Nine (Advanced)

A) What is the name of the joint where the leg and foot come together?

B) What has a basket and is used for flying?

C) Which animal has one or two humps on its back?

D) What is it called when two people sing together at the same time?

E) What is the hair above a person's eye called?

F) What is it called when something is your most liked?

G) What is a yellow metal that is used for jewelry and is usually very expensive?

H) If you do not want your friends to find you, what game are you playing?

I) Which measurement is the same as 2.54 centimetres?

J) Where is a place with many trees?   Tarzan lived there.

K) What is the name for a baby cat?

L) What is usually on the top of a bottle or jar?

M) Which planet is nearest the Sun?

N) What does a nurse use to give a patient an injection or blood test?

O) Which vegetable sometimes makes people cry when they slice it in the kitchen?

P) What do kings and queens usually live in?

Q) What do we call an old style pen, which is made from a big feather?

R) Which word means come back or go back?

S) Which family word describes a woman's husband's sister?

T) Which long thing do people often use to look at stars and see them better?

U) Where do many people study before getting a job?

V) What is quite similar to a mountain and has lava inside?

W) What do birds use to help them fly?

X, Y) Which musical instrument begins with 'x'?

Z) Who was the Greek king of the gods?

A-Z Quiz Ten (Advanced)

A) Who is white and female, has wings and can fly but is not an animal?   Some people think she comes from God.

B) What does a man have when he has thick hair over his chin, cheeks and neck?

C) What is the direction called when someone moves around in the same direction as a clock?

D) What are people sometimes called if they have no legs, no arms or a different physical problem?

E) Sport, running and walking are examples of what?

F) What is the Moon called when we can see all of it?

G) What do we sometimes call a very, very smart or intelligent person?

H) What is a person who does one or more special things such as saving a person from dying called?   Many movies have at least one of these people.

I) What is the name of a large Asian country with more than one billion people?

J) What kind of exercise sees people run slowly outside?

K) What do people often use for cutting?

L) What is another name for a young sheep?

M) What do people often look in to see their faces?

N) What special name do people call January 1st?

O) What is the name for a kind of musical drama?   Sydney has a famous house for this type of music.

P) What kind of person sometimes steals money or does other bad things at sea?

Q) What is the name of the country beginning with the letter 'q' but without a letter 'u' in its name?

R) What do many people wear on their fingers?

S) Which word means to eat or drink something in one, without biting or chewing it?

T) What are an elephant's two long teeth called?

U) If car drivers want to change direction in the middle of the road, what can they sometimes do?

V) What is the name of a team sport, in which a team can touch the ball three times before hitting it over a net?

W) What is it called when someone talks in a very quiet voice?   Sometimes people do this when they stand near to a person's ear and tell a secret.

X, Y) What word is used by children to describe bad tasting foods or drinks?

Z) What is another word for spots?

2

Categories Game

Categories Game

Use this game as a fun way for students to practise vocabulary over a wide range of subjects. Give students a colour or felt tip pen before the round starts and as soon as the time finishes take the pen away and ask students to write their points in pencil or biro. Allow the students about five or six minutes to read each topic heading and write just one answer per box. Have the timer visible if possible, and regularly remind the students of the remaining time.

Students or teams score two points for a right answer that no-one else has, one point if they have a right answer but another team has the same answer, and no points for no answer or a wrong answer. The maximum score for one round is normally eighteen points. Before playing the game with a class for the first time, clearly explain and illustrate the points system and encourage them to try to think of answers that other students will not have.

As the students try to fill in their answer sheet, they may encounter some questions they are not sure of. The teacher has many options. For the category, 'An odd number between sixty and seventy' (see page 33), many students might understand between sixty and seventy but not know what an odd number is. In this situation, the teacher can encourage them to guess, and then explain or ask other students to explain what an odd number is after the time is up. If the category is, 'A word that starts and finishes with the same letter' (see page 33) and many students do not understand, the teacher can perhaps write a_____a, b_____b, t_____t on the board as an illustration of how to answer. For some questions though, especially if only one team is struggling, the teacher will just have to tell the students to think some more or take a guess.

At the end of a round, the teacher asks every team in turn to say their answer for each question and awards points as stated above. The team with the most points wins the round. If time permits, students will probably want to play an additional round. Students work very well together in this game and playing in teams of about four or five is recommended.

Categories Game 1 (Lower Intermediate)

Read the categories and write one answer in each box.

A colour.	A weather word.	A family word.
A word starting with the letter 'a'.	**A body part.**	**A drink.**
Something green.	**A toy.**	**A word starting with the letter 's'.**

Categories Game 2 (Lower Intermediate)

Read the categories and write one answer in each box.

An animal.	An English boy's name.	An English girl's name.
A word starting with the letter 'b'.	A day of the week.	A shape.
Something very big.	A food.	A word starting with the letter 'd'.

Categories Game 3 (Upper Intermediate)

Read the categories and write one answer in each box.

A long food.	Something smaller than a plastic cup.	A colour of the rainbow.
Something you can see in the sky.	A body part below the neck.	Something in this classroom.
Something that lives in water.	An English girl's name beginning with a letter from 'a' to 'h'	A word starting with the letter 'z'.

Categories Game 4 (Upper Intermediate)

Read the categories and write one answer in each box.

A month after April and before October.	Something bigger than a classroom.	A flower name.
Something you can see at a park.	A body part above the neck.	Something you may see in a bedroom.
A farm animal.	An English boy's name beginning with a letter from 'a' to 'h'.	A word starting with the letter 'j'.

Categories Game 5 (Upper Intermediate)

Read the categories and write one answer in each box.

A month after October and before April.	A popular food on a hot day.	Something in a pencil case.
A sport name.	A body part that you only have one of.	Something you may see in a kitchen.
A zoo animal.	An English boy's name beginning with a letter from 'i' to 'p'.	A word starting with the letter 'v'.

Categories Game 6 (Upper Intermediate)

Read the categories and write one answer in each box.

A green vegetable.	A drink that most children like.	A country in Europe.
A total you can get if you roll two dice together.	A body part that you have more than one of.	Something you may see in a bathroom.
A popular house pet.	An English boy's name beginning with a letter from 'q' to 'z'.	A word starting with the letter 'k'.

Categories Game 7 (Upper Intermediate)

Read the categories and write one answer in each box.

A vegetable that is not green.	A game or sport that uses a ball.	A season.
Something with wheels.	An elementary school subject.	Something you may see in a living room.
Something scary.	An English girl's name beginning with a letter from 'i' to 'p'.	A word starting with the letter 'u'.

Categories Game 8 (Upper Intermediate)

Read the categories and write one answer in each box.

A popular summer fruit.	Something you can see inside a car.	A musical instrument.
Something people can read other than a book.	Something most people do in the first hour after getting up in the morning.	Something many people wear on a snowy day.
A popular picnic food.	An English girl's name beginning with a letter from 'q' to 'z'.	A word starting with the letter 'i'.

Categories Game 9 (Advanced)

Read the categories and write one answer in each box.

An example of a word that starts and finishes with the same letter.	A reason to see a doctor.	Something that uses electricity.
A musical instrument with strings.	An odd number between sixty and seventy (write the word, not the number).	A country in South America.
Something people wear other than clothes.	A reason a teacher punishes a student.	A kind of natural disaster.

Categories Game 10 (Advanced)

Read the categories and write one answer in each box.

A word that has ten letters or more (correct spelling).	A name of a planet other than Earth.	A special day of the year.
A musical wind instrument.	An even number higher than eighty and lower than ninety (write the word, not the number).	A country in Africa.
An internal body organ.	A reason for the police arresting somebody.	An animal that lives underground.

3

5, 4, 3, 2, 1 Game

5, 4, 3, 2, 1 Game

Use this game to practise the students' listening skills and vocabulary. This is the only section in the book for which students do not receive a handout or worksheet to use or fill in.

Put the students into teams of about four or five students and give each team one board and a marker, or paper and colour pen. Tell the students the subject for the game such as jobs or musical instruments. If the students are playing the game for the first time, clearly explain that the five point clue is more difficult than the four point hint and the four point clue is more challenging than the three point hint and so on. When everyone is ready, read the five point hint for the first round a couple of times and then start a countdown from ten to one. Within this time, students quietly discuss the answer with their team and then quickly write it on their board or paper. After the time is up, quickly count, "One, two, three!" and make each team lift its answer up. Read or ask each team to read its answer out loud and then reveal (using suspense if desired!) whether any team has the right answer. Right answers score five points for the round and then the teacher moves onto the second question.

If no teams have the correct answer, ask them to erase their answer board or cross out their previous answers and give the four point clue (perhaps reminding teams of the five point hint at the same time) and continue in the same way as before. Any right answers earn four points but if no team matches the answer, continue all the way down to one point or until a team matches the right answer. Write the points for each round on the main class board as you go along, continuing the game until all six questions have been completed or no time remains. The team with the most points in total is the winner.

Take steps to avoid misconceptions some students have before becoming fully used to the game. Some students sometimes fail to realize that the four point hint is connected to the previous five point hint after a wrong answer so explain that clearly. Also some teams will write answers that were already revealed to be wrong during earlier clues so highlight that clearly the first time it happens.

5, 4, 3, 2, 1 Jobs Game

What is my job?	What is my job?
5) I have to stand up a lot.	5) I work outside.
4) Sometimes I am kind but sometimes I am angry.	4) I often continue working when I am very old.
3) I work very hard.	3) I usually eat fresh food.
2) I see children every day.	2) I am often poor.
1) I work in a classroom.	1) I see many animals.
Teacher	farmer
What is my job?	**What is my job?**
5) I meet many people.	5) I see many people.
4) I have to talk a lot.	4) I help people all day, especially after breakfast.
3) I visit other countries.	3) If I make a big mistake, people could die.
2) My job is very important.	2) I am usually a man.
1) I am the leader of a country.	1) I help people travel but not on the roads.
President	Train driver
What is my job?	**What is my job?**
5) I work in a special room.	5) I need good ideas.
4) I wear white clothes.	4) I often have to change my work before finishing.
3) I often try new things.	3) I can work at home.
2) I sometimes give medicines to animals.	2) I need a pen or pencil and usually a computer.
1) I sometimes become famous.	1) You can see my work in a library.
Scientist	Writer

5, 4, 3, 2, 1 Food Game

What food am I?	**What food am I?**
5) I am boiled in water.	5) I can be eaten cooked or uncooked.
4) In some countries, people eat me every day.	4) I am long.
3) I can be eaten with many different foods.	3) I am a vegetable.
2) I am a healthy food.	2) Rabbits like me.
1) I am white.	1) I am orange.
What food am I?	**What food am I?**
5) I need a sauce to taste good.	5) I can be any shape but usually I am round or square.
4) I am long.	4) I am eaten on happy days.
3) I am boiled in water.	3) I usually have cream or chocolate on top of me.
2) I am difficult to pick up.	2) I have candles on me.
1) I am from Italy.	1) I am eaten on birthdays.
What food am I?	**What food am I?**
5) I come in many varieties.	5) In some countries, people grow me in their gardens.
4) I am not eaten at dinner.	4) I am usually small.
3) I am eaten with a spoon.	3) I am popular in the summer.
2) I am eaten with milk.	2) I am sometimes in milkshakes or on cakes.
1) I am eaten at breakfast.	1) I am red.

5, 4, 3, 2, 1 Musical Instruments Game

What instrument am I?	What instrument am I?
5) I am smaller than a piano.	5) I am noisier than a violin.
4) I am quieter than a guitar.	4) I am bigger than a tambourine.
3) My shape is very different to most other instruments.	3) I am important for rock music.
2) I am very easy to play.	2) You can hit me with a stick or with your hands.
1) I have three sides.	1) I am round.
What instrument am I?	**What instrument am I?**
5) I am smaller than a guitar.	5) I am heavier than a drum.
4) People can sit down or stand up to play me.	4) I am bigger than a harp.
3) I have metal jingles in my sides.	3) Sometimes people sing when they play me.
2) I am very easy to play.	2) I am in almost every school.
1) I am round.	1) I have black and white keys.
What instrument am I?	**What instrument am I?**
5) I am smaller than a piano.	5) I am lighter than a trumpet.
4) I am longer than a recorder.	4) You hold me with two hands.
3) I have an on and off button.	3) I have many holes.
2) I have many different sounds.	2) You blow air into me.
1) I look like a small piano.	1) Young children often learn how to play me.

5, 4, 3, 2, 1 Places Game

What place am I?	What place am I?
5) I am very busy every day.	5) I am in almost every town.
4) People sometimes wait for a long time inside me.	4) I am closed on Sundays.
3) You usually take a ticket when you come to me.	3) Customers usually only stay here for a few minutes.
2) People from many countries use me.	2) People write addresses on envelopes here.
1) I have many airplanes.	1) You can send letters and parcels to people here.
What place am I?	**What place am I?**
5) I am often very big.	5) There are not usually many people here.
4) People often come here at weekends or at night.	4) I am usually very big.
3) People sing or shout here.	3) This place is often smelly.
2) You can see two teams here.	2) You can see grass here.
1) The teams kick a ball here.	1) You can see animals such as cows and sheep here.
What place am I?	**What place am I?**
5) You can buy food here.	5) Anyone can come here.
4) People come here with their friends.	4) Sometimes schools come here.
3) Young people like to come here.	3) You change your clothes here.
2) You sit down and talk here.	2) You can see water here.
1) People drink coffee here.	1) You can swim here.

5, 4, 3, 2, 1 Animals Game

What animal am I?	**What animal am I?**
5) I sometimes kill humans.	5) I am a small animal.
4) I am long.	4) I eat grass.
3) I live in water.	3) I am often a pet.
2) I am green.	2) Foxes sometimes eat me.
1) I am similar to an alligator.	1) I have big ears.
Crocodile	*rabbit.*
What animal am I?	**What animal am I?**
5) I am bigger than a sheep.	5) I am quieter than a dog.
4) I am stronger than most other animals.	4) I am smaller than a cat.
3) I usually live in Africa or Asia.	3) You can hold me in your hand.
2) I look slow.	2) Scientists test medicines on me.
1) I have a long trunk.	1) Cats like to eat me.
Elephant	*mouse*
What animal am I?	**What animal am I?**
5) I have four legs.	5) I am more dangerous than a cat.
4) I am faster than a cow.	4) I eat meat.
3) I often live for about twenty-five years.	3) I don't have legs.
2) I was a very important animal before cars were invented.	2) I am long.
1) I can sleep standing up.	1) I make a hissing sound.
horse	*Snake*

5, 4, 3, 2, 1 Sports Game

What sport am I?	**What sport am I?**
5) You have to run fast.	5) I am an Olympic sport.
4) I am sometimes dangerous.	4) You do not wear a t-shirt and shorts for this sport.
3) Players throw a ball.	3) You have to race.
2) Diamonds are important.	2) You often wear something special on your face.
1) American teams are very good at this sport.	1) You do this sport in water.
What sport am I?	**What sport am I?**
5) I am played outside.	5) I have a ball.
4) I have a ball.	4) My ball is smaller than a baseball.
3) I am often played near trees, sand and water.	3) You use a bat.
2) You walk a lot but you do not usually run.	2) I am played inside.
1) This sport has small holes in the ground.	1) You play me on a table.
What sport am I?	**What sport am I?**
5) I am a team sport.	5) I am an individual sport.
4) You have to wear lots of clothes to protect your body.	4) I do not use a ball.
3) There are two goals.	3) I am a dangerous sport.
2) I am an indoor sport.	2) You have to wear gloves.
1) I am played on ice.	1) You have to try and hit your opponent.

5, 4, 3, 2, 1 Household Objects Game

Name the household object	Name the household object
5) You turn it on and off. 4) It is often in a high place. 3) People often use it early in the morning or at night. 2) It is in the bathroom. 1) Water comes out of it.	5) It is not usually in the bathroom or kitchen. 4) Very old people do not usually use it. 3) It is expensive. 2) You switch it on and off. 1) It has the internet.
Name the household object	Name the household object
5) It is usually a rectangular shape. 4) It is expensive. 3) It helps us do something faster. 2) It is usually in the kitchen. 1) It can be used to make food hot for a second time.	5) It is big. 4) Many houses have more than one. 3) It is not used much in the afternoon. 2) It is in the bedroom. 1) It is used for sleeping.
Name the household object	Name the household object
5) You can see many of these things in most houses. 4) You can often see them in the living room or kitchen. 3) They are not big. 2) You have to wash them. 1) You put tea or coffee in them.	5) You use it every day. 4) It is not big. 3) Children and adults use different sizes. 2) You use it in the bathroom. 1) You use it to brush your teeth.

5, 4, 3, 2, 1 In the Supermarket Game

What am I?	**What am I?**
5) Many people buy me every time they go to the supermarket. 4) I am a drink. 3) My colour is white. 2) Babies like me. 1) I usually come from a cow.	5) I am cheap. 4) I am small. 3) You put me in your mouth. 2) I often have a fruity taste. 1) People usually do not swallow me.
What am I?	**What am I?**
5) People use me every day. 4) I am often white but I can also be different colours. 3) I am soft. 2) I am usually in the bathroom. 1) You use me when you go to the toilet.	5) You can buy me cheaply in the supermarket. 4) I am free in some other places. 3) I am very important for your health. 2) You drink me. 1) I am always in your body.
What am I?	**What am I?**
5) Children often like me. 4) I am big. 3) I am in most supermarkets but you cannot buy me. 2) I have wheels. 1) You put your shopping in me.	5) I am very big. 4) I help people shop comfortably. 3) You cannot buy me. 2) I am outside the supermarket. 1) You leave your car here.

5, 4, 3, 2, 1 Countries Game

Which country am I?	**Which country am I?**
5) Yellow is one of the colours on my flag. 4) I am a big country. 3) I am in Asia. 2) I have a famous wall. 1) Red is an important colour for my country.	5) People like to dance in this country. 4) I am a big country. 3) I am good at soccer. 2) I am in South America. 1) My flag is yellow and green.
Which country am I?	**Which country am I?**
5) I am a cold country. 4) I am in Europe. 3) I am near Sweden. 2) My flag is white and blue. 1) You might see Santa here.	5) I am a European country. 4) I have more than one name. 3) My people usually speak English well. 2) I have beautiful tulips. 1) I border Belgium.
Which country am I?	**Which country am I?**
5) English is not my first language. 4) I have a president. 3) My currency is the Euro. 2) You might see Mickey Mouse here. 1) I have a very famous tower.	5) People can ski here. 4) Art and music are important in this country. 3) My flag has three colours. 2) I am in Europe. 1) People eat pizza and spaghetti here.

5, 4, 3, 2, 1 Clothing and Accessories Game

What am I?	**What am I?**
5) Anyone can wear me.	5) Men do not often wear me.
4) You wear me on the top half of your body.	4) People often take me off before playing sport.
3) I am often worn in winter.	3) I am usually small.
2) I am often made from wool.	2) I am sometimes made of gold.
1) I go around your neck.	1) You wear me in your ear.
What am I?	**What am I?**
5) Old people do not wear me.	5) I am worn by men more than women.
4) I can be worn in spring, summer, autumn or winter.	4) I am expensive.
3) People wear me in the day time more than at night.	3) I am worn in the day more than at night.
2) Boys and girls wear me.	2) I am often black or grey.
1) I am worn at school.	1) Businessmen wear me.
What am I?	**What am I?**
5) I am worn in any season.	5) Almost everybody wears me.
4) I am worn in any weather.	4) People wear me in the day time more than at night.
3) I am often expensive.	3) People wear me less in the summer.
2) Some people wear me all day and never take me off.	2) I am smelly.
1) Married people often wear me.	1) You wear me on your foot.

4

Anagrams

Anagrams

Unscramble the letters to reveal the words. Use these exercises to practise vocabulary and spelling, and for reviewing learning in previous lessons. They may also be used to introduce limited amounts of new vocabulary. Only give these anagram exercises to your students if they are already likely to know or be able to work out the majority of the vocabulary items so that they can feel an element of achievement at the same time as they learn some new words.

For topics such as days of the week and months, capital letters have not been used amongst the mixed up letters. Students should correctly use capital letters in addition to unscrambling the words. The exercise containing anagrams about Space are more challenging and thus the appropriate capital letters have been provided as hints. Where an answer contains two words, the letters for each word have been separated to enable each word to be solved without becoming overly difficult e.g. 'etj isking' becomes 'jet skiing' (see page 55). Additionally there are a small number of three word answers, which follow the same method e.g. 'layping het opani' becomes 'playing the piano' (see page 54).

For certain categories such as hobbies, transport, feelings, drinks or vegetables, early finishers can be asked to try and think of at least one other vocabulary item of their own and make an anagram for it. The teacher or student could then write the extra anagrams clearly on the class board for the whole class to attempt to solve.

Anagrams 1 (Days of the Week)

Rearrange the letters to make the days of the week.

Use a capital letter and write the correct answers.

andmoy	
suetady	
addeenswy	
yadsruht	
fairyd	
aadrstuy	
usyand	
odaty	
readystey	
ooomrrtw	

Anagrams 2 (Months)

Rearrange the letters to make the months of the year.

Use a capital letter, write the correct months and the month number.

eunj	June	6
yam		
jyul		
prail		
charm		
staguu		
robotce		
embcdeer		
beertemps		
anajury		
movebern		
yraurbef		

Anagrams 3 (Feelings and Emotions)

Rearrange the letters to find some words describing feelings and emotions.
Write the correct answers.

paphy	
das	
ganry	
dirte	
skic	
bdeor	
carsed	
cdeeitx	
wdeiorr	
deiprrssu	

Anagrams 4 (Drinks)

Rearrange the letters to find the names of some drinks.

Write the correct answers.

eat	
limk	
aclo	
newi	
ebre	
retaw	
ffcoee	
adeelmno	
shakklime	
norage cijue	

Anagrams 5 (Vegetables)

Rearrange the letters to find the names of some vegetables.

Write the correct answers.

ape	
norc	
oonni	
acorrt	
eepppr	
pattoo	
abcabeg	
pinkpum	
rebmuccu	
mmoorshu	

Anagrams 6 (Hobbies)

Rearrange the letters to make some common hobbies.

Write the correct answers.

owlbing	
inglapy intens	
pinginat	
layping het opani	
inplagy notnimdab	
wingmmis	
pglnaiy ballstekab	
nogokic	
planigy retupcom emags	
doingstarbake	

Anagrams 7 (Dangerous and Scary Activities)

Rearrange the letters to make some dangerous and scary activities.
Write the correct answers.

kingis	
etj isking	
geebun jpum	
paacehrtu jmup	
abcsu viding	
bullitingfgh	
rcok ingcimbl	
ingonboardsw	
rollcatseerro	
caningoe	

Anagrams 8 (Space)

Rearrange the letters to make some words about planets and Space.

Write the correct answers.

O.U.F.	
purJeit	
arMs	
hEart	
artSun	
curryMe	
usneV	
penteNu	
sunraU	
Teh onoM	

Anagrams 9 (Forms of Transport A)

Rearrange the letters to make some forms of transport.

Write the correct answers.

rac	
usb	
nav	
abot	
xati	
rolry	
raint	
uckrt	
busyaw	
bcceily	

Anagrams 10 (Forms of Transport B)

Rearrange the letters to make some forms of transport.

Write the correct answers.

acone	
cooster	
ecilop arc	
efir eennig	
heretcopil	
robotmike	
carttor	
abcelmnua	
incycleu	
dubleo drecke sub	

5

Wordsearches

Wordsearches

Use these exercises to practise words and spelling, review learning in previous lessons, and introduce new vocabulary items. To ensure the students focus on the key points, most words are fairly easy to find quickly. The majority of the words are in horizontal and vertical directions, with a few diagonally too. Some words are back to front. The puzzles present varied and interesting vocabulary, with a wide range of challenges such as matching monuments, cities or nationalities to countries, and animal sounds to the correct animals. Other tasks require students to identify, find and write opposites or homophones. In the irregular verbs wordsearch, students are also required to attempt to write sentences using the target word to stretch them further. Some of the activities do not give wordlists, making the students use their knowledge or look for the hints hidden in the puzzles such as capital letters. As a further challenge, the number of words is not given in the weather wordsearch.

The completed activities can be used as a stimulus for further discussion or study. For instance, the world cities puzzle invites students to talk about where each city is. Ask the students whether they can think of additional vocabulary such as more homophones or natural disasters. What is an earthquake? Who can draw a simple picture of a flood on the board? What famous monuments are in their country? Do they know any other animal sounds in English? Are they curious about the sounds made by different animals? What sound does a rooster make?! There are a massive number of other opposite pairs other than those in the puzzle. How many can they think of?

Wordsearch 1 (Natural Disasters)

Look for the ten disasters and write each word one more time after finding them.

e	a	r	t	h	q	u	a	k	e
f	v	d	r	o	u	g	h	t	n
f	a	m	i	n	e	r	o	s	a
b	l	i	z	z	a	r	d	u	c
f	a	z	z	z	n	e	s	n	i
l	n	i	i	a	i	m	u	a	r
o	c	b	d	k	s	l	e	m	r
o	h	o	n	u	l	e	b	i	u
d	e	n	o	l	c	y	c	o	h

avalanche	
blizzard	
cyclone	
drought	
earthquake	
famine	
flood	
hurricane	
tornado	
tsunami	

Wordsearch 2 (World Cities)

Find these famous world cities and then talk about which countries they are in.

L	o	n	d	o	n	T	g
o	o	P	a	r	o	o	n
n	R	o	a	k	d	o	i
d	o	o	y	r	m	k	j
e	e	o	m	a	i	y	i
S	y	d	n	e	y	s	e
t	s	e	p	a	d	u	B
u	o	e	S	e	o	u	l

Beijing
Budapest
London
Paris
Rome
Seoul
Sydney
Tokyo

Wordsearch 3 (Soccer World Cup Winners)

Find eight soccer (football) World Cup winners and then write the name of each country in the box below.

i	y	a	u	g	u	r	U	o
t	n	E	n	g	l	a	n	d
a	a	S	p	a	i	n	e	I
l	m	x	q	z	o	e	c	t
A	r	g	e	n	t	i	n	a
m	e	g	e	r	m	a	a	l
e	G	e	r	m	y	n	r	y
r	B	r	a	z	i	l	F	o

Wordsearch 4 (Famous Monuments)

Read the names of the monuments, write the country they are in and then find the country names in the wordsearch.

A	u	s	t	r	a	l	i	a
m	E	n	g	l	a	n	d	o
e	g	d	n	I	n	d	i	a
r	y	I	t	a	l	y	t	d
i	p	q	e	e	n	s	n	a
c	t	r	o	m	d	i	f	n
a	G	r	e	e	c	e	h	a
r	b	e	c	n	a	r	F	C

Acropolis of Athens	Greece
Ayers Rock and Sydney Opera House	
Big Ben and Stonehenge	
Colosseum and Leaning Tower of Pisa	
Eiffel Tower	
The Great Wall of _____	
Niagara Falls	
Pyramids	
Statue of Liberty	
Taj Mahal	

Wordsearch 5 (Nationalities)

Write the names of the natives from each country and find the words.

A	m	e	r	i	c	a	n
S	I	t	a	l	i	a	n
w	e	s	e	n	i	h	C
i	s	w	i	d	i	h	h
s	y	n	a	l	a	t	i
s	E	n	g	l	i	s	h
J	a	p	a	n	e	s	e
C	h	c	n	e	r	F	o

America	American
Canada	
China	
England	
France	
Italy	
Japan	
Switzerland	

Wordsearch 6 (Animal Sounds)

Find the animal sounds and then write the name of the animal that makes each sound.

b	a	a	t	o	e	z	w
n	m	i	a	o	w	o	c
c	l	u	c	k	o	a	h
m	j	k	l	f	m	s	i
t	i	b	b	i	r	o	r
n	e	i	g	h	p	i	p
s	q	u	e	a	k	n	o
u	s	q	u	a	c	k	e

baa	sheep
chirp	
cluck	
miaow	
neigh	
oink	
quack	
ribbit	
squeak	
woof	

Wordsearch 7 (Opposites)

Write the opposites and then find them.

o	l	n	i	c	t	o	y
a	i	e	b	d	t	o	r
t	g	d	e	z	u	s	i
t	h	i	n	n	p	a	m
u	t	s	g	l	r	f	e
o	n	t	b	s	a	e	s
h	m	u	m	l	a	z	s
s	h	o	r	t	e	d	y

long	
neat	
fat	
inside	
old	
hard-working	
dangerous	
dark	

Wordsearch 8 (Weather)

Look for weather words.   When you find a word, write it in the left box and then quickly draw a matching picture in the right box.   How many words can you find?

l	i	g	h	t	n	i	n	g
c	x	y	z	s	u	n	n	y
o	a	b	r	a	i	n	y	d
l	c	f	o	g	g	y	d	u
d	e	f	g	h	i	j	k	o
i	l	m	w	i	n	d	y	l
c	n	o	p	q	r	s	t	c
y	s	n	o	w	y	h	o	t

Wordsearch 9 (Irregular Verbs)

Write the past simple tense, find it, and make a sentence for each word.

z	y	x	w	v	u	d	q
b	o	u	g	h	t	r	u
t	e	a	t	h	j	a	a
n	a	n	o	f	k	n	p
e	a	u	l	f	l	k	a
w	x	e	g	r	e	s	i
i	w	u	m	h	o	l	d
e	m	a	c	n	t	l	t

buy	bought	I bought a present for my friend.
come		
drink		
feel		
fly		
go		
pay		
teach		

Wordsearch 10 (Homophones)

A homophone is a word that sounds the same as another word but is spelt differently. Write the homophones, draw a small picture of the new word in the box and then find the homophones in the wordsearch.

x	s	u	n	t	r	o	e	m
y	e	r	h	e	m	n	i	n
z	c	g	w	o	p	e	g	e
q	i	o	b	e	a	r	h	d
n	l	d	f	g	h	j	t	r
f	s	w	i	t	c	h	o	e
a	q	w	e	r	t	y	y	e
b	c	d	e	f	s	e	a	d

son	sun	☼
ate	eight	8
see		
knight		
which		
dear		
bare		
flour		

6

Crosswords

Crosswords

Solve the clues to complete the puzzles. Use these exercises to consolidate students' knowledge of nouns, verbs, and correct word choices in sentences. Four crosswords devoted to daily actions and weekend activities are presented as fill in the blanks so that students can practise using particular nouns and verbs in context.

When doing the Numbers crossword (see page 78), students should insert hyphens into the grid squares where necessary. For example, clue one across has ten squares allocated for the answer of twenty-six. Words without vowels (see page 79) will help bring students attention to the fact that almost all words must have at least one of the five vowels in and if they do not, they will almost certainly use the letter 'y' – sometimes known as 'the sixth vowel'. * The three crosswords devoted to the challenging topic of phrasal verbs are most suited to higher level learners and the teacher may need to provide a few hints as the students work through those puzzles.

Give a copy to each student. Students can study these tasks individually but working in pairs often works particularly well. Students could discuss every clue together and write the answers or work mainly alone but compare answers with each other and try and work out challenging clues together. They can also discuss spellings of difficult words. Allow them to check spelling with the teacher too. If many students are struggling with just one or two clues left, the teacher could let student pairs double up with other pairs nearby to try and complete the crossword.

If the crossword is likely to be challenging for the level of the children, groups could be increased to three or four students per group. Give enough time for most students to finish and then go through the answers as a class. One method of doing these crosswords that is popular with the students is to present them as a speed game. The first pair to finish with the correct answers wins. Points, stickers or other prizes can sometimes also be given for second and third places.

_____

* Exceptions to this are abbreviations, and also certain scrabble words, which the typical ESL or EFL learners are unlikely to ever need.

Crossword (Before School)

Read the clues and write the answers.

Across →

    1.   Get ____ (out of bed).

    4.   Put your school _____ on.

    5.   Eat _____.

    7.   Take a _____.

    8.   _____ your face.

    9.   _____ dressed.

Down ↓

    2.   _____ your shoes on.

    3.   _____ juice or water.

    6. Brush your _____.

    8.   _____ up (open your eyes).

Crossword (After School)

Read the clues and write the answers.

Across ⟶

2.   _____ changed (clothes).

3.   _____ books.

6.   Play with _____s.

7.   Do your _____.

8.   _____ to music.

Down ↓

1.   Wash the _____.

2.   Play computer _____.

4.   Eat _____.

5.   _____ television.

6.   Talk to your _____.

Crossword (Before Sleeping)

Read the clues and write the answers.

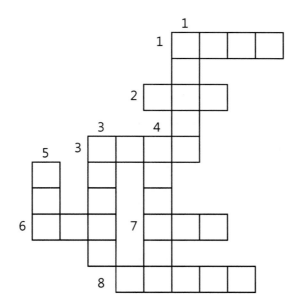

Across ➔

1. Read a _____.
2. _____ your pyjamas on.
3. _____ your face.
6. _____ supper.
7. Switch the light _____.
8. _____ your eyes.

Down ↓

1. _____ your teeth.
3. _____ your diary.
4. Pack your _____ bag.
5. _____ down in bed.

Crossword (At the Weekend)

Read the clues and write the answers.

Across →

1. _____ on a trip.
3. Watch _____.
5. Jog, walk, run or play sport.   Make your body healthier.
6. _____ a movie.
8. Go _____ (Buy things).

Down ↓

1. _____ up late.
2. Go on a _____.
4. _____ your grandma and grandpa.
7. Do your _____.
9. _____ soccer.

Crossword (Life of a Baby)

Read the clues and write the answers.

Across ➞

2. Move around on the floor (before walking).

5. Usually born in a _____.

6. Start _____. (Say words).

9. Wear a _____. (British people say, 'nappy'. What do Americans say?).

Down ↓

1. _____ over.

2. When water comes from the eyes.

3. Start _____. (Next stage after crawling).

4. Zzzzz.

7. A daytime sleep.

8. _____ milk.

Crossword (Numbers)

Read the clues and write the answers.

Across →

1. How many letters are in the alphabet?
2. How many sides does a rhombus have?
4. How many hours are in one day?
8. What is seventeen minus six?

Down ↓

1. How many days are in January?
3. Which number is smaller than one?
4. If a woman has twins, how many babies does she have?
5. How many legs does a spider have?
6. How many wheels does a tricycle have?
7. How many toes do most people have?

Crossword (Words Without Vowels)

Most English words have at least one vowel (a, e, i, o, u).

However, this crossword does not have any vowels.

Read the clues and write the answers.

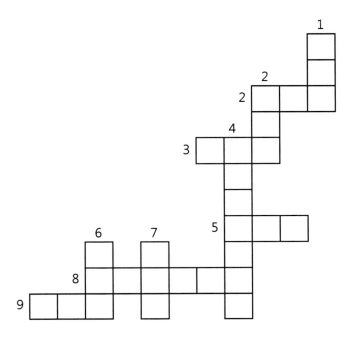

Across

2. What do you see if you go outside and look up?

3. What is the opposite of wet?

5. Attempt or test something.

8. In music what is a repeated sound called?   It can be fast, slow or normal.

9. Think of a question word, starting with 'w'.

Down

1. What do some people do when they are very sad or in a lot of pain?

2. What are quiet or nervous people sometimes called?

4. Same answer as number eight across but add an 's'.

6. Think of a cooking style used for bacon, eggs, and sometimes rice.

7. Where do many students have P.E. class?   The word is short for gymnasium.

Crossword (Phrasal Verbs 1)

Read the clues and write the answers.

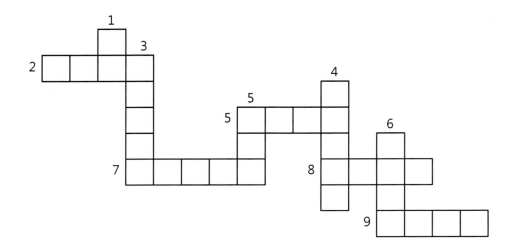

Across ⟶

2. _____ up (when a child gets bigger and older).

5. _____ up (make the sound on a television, computer or stereo louder).

7. _____ up (do something quickly).

8. _____ back (telephone someone after he or she telephoned you).

9. _____ up (clean the dirty dishes after cooking and eating).

Down ↓

1. ____ out (leave the house, visit somewhere, head for a different place).

3. _____ out (be careful)!

4. _____ out (hit someone and make them unconscious, especially in boxing).

5. _____ on (wear clothes in a shop to check whether they are good to buy).

6. _____ up (put a party balloon in your mouth and make it big).

Crossword (Phrasal Verbs 2)

Read the clues and write the answers.

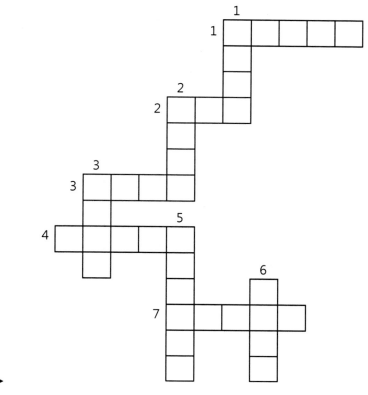

Across →

1. _____ up (get up out of your chair).
2. _____ up (time to get out of bed).
3. _____ after (look like someone in your family or have the same character).
4. _____ up (wear nice clothes when going out).
7. _____ away (put trash or garbage into a trash can or wastebasket).

Down ↓

1. _____ up! ("Be quiet!" – a bit rude or unkind).
2. _____ up (stop trying to do something – maybe because it is too difficult).
3. _____ down (make the sound on a computer, television or stereo quieter).
5. _____ off (stop using lights, computer, television, radio etc.).
6. _____ in (make something look bigger or nearer when using a camera).

Crossword (Phrasal Verbs 3)

Read the clues and write the answers.

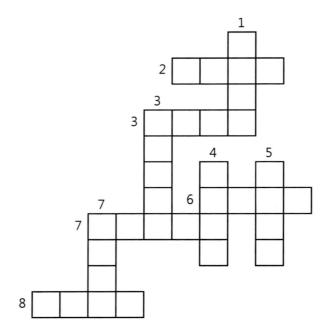

Across →

2. _____ forward to (be excited about something that will happen soon).

3. _____ out (flowers do this in the spring).

6. Pass _____ (a different way to say, 'die').

7. _____ up (stop seeing a boyfriend or girlfriend and split up).

8. _____ out (get information about something).

Down ↓

1. _____ in (leave your old house and start living in a new house).

3. _____ down (when a shop or business finishes work for the very last time).

4. _____ up (open your eyes after sleeping).

5. _____ up (stop spending money, put it together and buy something later).

7. _____ down (when fire makes a building fall to the ground and destroys it).

7

Mystery Word

Mystery Word

Write the answer to each question horizontally in the appropriate boxes. Find every answer to reveal and write a mystery word related to the topic. Use these exercises to give students opportunities to practise reading and understanding, and vocabulary and spelling.

The first seven puzzles are suitable for all intermediate level learners, although there may be the odd question for which they require additional hints or guidance to solve. The final three puzzles contain longer words and are aimed more specifically at advanced learners. The vocabulary will challenge them in some cases and they may need some further clues on occasions. Many will also find the spelling difficult and might require additional support.

Give a sheet to each student. Students can study these tasks individually but working in pairs often works particularly well. Students could discuss every clue together and write the answers, or work mainly alone but compare answers with each other and try and work out challenging clues together. They can also discuss spellings of difficult words. Allow them to check spelling with the teacher too. If many students are struggling with just one or two clues left, the teacher could let student pairs double up with other pairs nearby to try and complete the puzzle. If the exercise is likely to be challenging for the level of the children, groups could be increased to three or four students per group from the start.

To successfully complete the puzzle, every clue must be solved and the mystery word identified. If the activity is being used competitively, such as in a first to finish style game, and no pairs or teams are able to complete the whole puzzle then the winners are the students who answer the most questions correctly and are able to work out the mystery word from the letters they have found. In games when students are able to answer all of the questions, the winners are the first to solve every clue, not the students who are able to guess the mystery word just from answering one or two of the questions.

Mystery Word (In the Bathroom)

Read the clues, write the answers and find the mystery word.

1)
2)
3)
4)
5)
6)
7)
8)
9)
10)

1) What do people use to dry their hands?

2) What do people use with water to wash their hands and faces?

3) What do people use to clean themselves when they are using the toilet? (Two words)

4) What do people sit on in the bathroom?

5) What do people use to wash their hair?

6) What do people hold and use to help clean the toilet or other parts of the bathroom?

7) What do we use to give us water to wash our whole body?

8) What do some people use instead of a shower? People can sit or lie in it.

9) Where do people wash their hands in the bathroom?

10) What comes in a tube and is used to help people brush their teeth?

What is the mystery word?

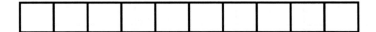

Mystery Word (In the Kitchen)

Read the clues, write the answers and find the mystery word.

1)

2)

3)

4)

5)

6)

7)

8)

9)

10)

1) What do people use to cook food?   It needs gas or electricity.

2) What word is used to describe everything people used when they ate dinner? (Wash the _____.)

3) What do people put soup or cereal in?

4) What do people usually use to eat ice cream or cereal?

5) What small round thing do many people put their cup of tea or coffee on?

6) What do people put their cooked food on?

7) What do people often have in their right hand when they eat?

8) What is used to make cooked food hot or warm again when it has gone cold?

9) What do people often have in their left hand when they eat?

10) Where do people wash the dishes?

What is the mystery word?

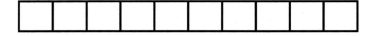

Mystery Word (In the Bedroom)

Read the clues, write the answers and find the mystery word.

1)
2)
3)
4)
5)
6)
7)
8)
9)

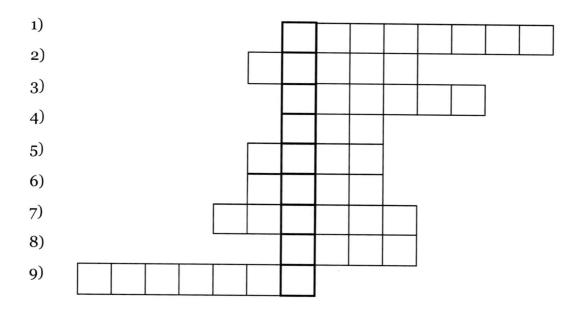

1) What do people use to play games, use the internet or do their homework?
2) What big thing is put on a bed to keep people warm?
3) What rectangular object is used on a bed to support the head when sleeping?
4) Where do people sleep?
5) What do children play with in a bedroom? (Plural)
6) What is the name of a small light often seen near a bed?
7) If you look at this, you see your own face.   What is it?
8) Where do people put a computer?   People also sit here to do their homework at home, or study at school.
9) What do many people, especially children, wear in bed?

What is the mystery word?

Mystery Word (In the Living Room)

Read the clues, write the answers and find the mystery word.

1)

2)

3)

4)

5)

6)

7)

8)

9)

1) What do people often put cups, books or newspapers on when they are not using them?

2) Where do many people put flowers?   It is often made from glass.

3) What do people use to see better in a living room?

4) Where do people often put all of their books?   It is often made from wood.

5) What is usually green and grows?   It will die without water.

6) What do people sit on?   You can also see this in a classroom.

7) What is the name of a comfortable chair often seen in a living room?

8) What do people use to keep cool on a hot day?

9) What do people use to listen to music?

What is the mystery word?

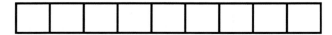

Mystery Word (Words with a letter X)

Read the clues, write the answers and find the mystery word.

1) What do people have when doctors want to photograph bones?

2) What is the name of a colourless gas that is part of the air?

3) Show how to do something.   Show a demonstration.   A teacher often shows one before students start studying.

4) Which animal is a kind of dog and is often hunted?

5) What is the opposite of cheap?

6) Give something to someone and receive something in return (change something).

7) In which dangerous sport do two people punch each other?

8) Fill in the blank: last week, this week, _____ week.

9) What is fifty minus thirty-four?

What is the mystery word?

Mystery Word (Fruit)

Read the clues, write the answers and find the mystery word.

1)
2)
3)
4)
5)
6)
7)
8)
9)
10)

1) Which fruit is small and brown on the outside, and green inside with black seeds?

2) What is round and usually green or red?   It is difficult to eat very quickly.

3) Which summer fruit is small and red and sometimes eaten with cream?

4) What is quite big with big leaves on top, difficult to cut and yellow inside?

5) What is green or purple, sold in bunches and used to make wine?   (Plural)

6) Which fruit is yellow and sour and is similar to an oval in shape?

7) Which fruit is the same colour as its name?

8) What is the name of a very small blue fruit?

9) Which tropical fruit can be red, yellow, green or orange, has a seed inside and is often sweet?

10) What is the name of the fruit, which monkeys like to eat?

What is the mystery word?

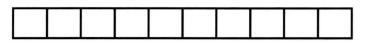

Mystery Word (On the Beach)

Read the clues, write the answers and find the mystery word.

1)
2)
3)
4)
5)
6)
7)
8)
9)
10)

1) Where do people go swimming on the beach?

2) What do many people wear over their eyes when it is sunny?

3) What do people walk on when they are on the beach?

4) What do people have when they are thirsty?

5) What has ten legs and lives in or near the sea? Some people eat this creature.

6) What do people use when they surf in the sea?

7) What is light and round, often made of plastic and thrown on a beach?

8) What do many people sit on when they are on the beach? They can also use it to get dry after going swimming in the sea.

9) What comes from animals and is often found on the beach near the sea?

10) What do we call the big, light ball often played with on a beach? (Two words)

What is the mystery word?

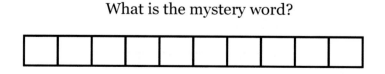

Mystery Word (Nine Letter Words)

Read the clues, write the answers and find the mystery word.

1)

2)

3)

4)

5)

6)

7)

8)

9)

1) Where do people go to buy books?

2) What is it called when someone counts, '5, 4, 3, 2, 1'?

3) Which popular food is usually brown, is often seen in or on the top of cakes and is also an ice cream flavour?

4) What is more than never but less than always or usually?

5) Which word means better than very good? Teachers sometimes say it to students if they do very well.

6) What is the leader called in many countries?

7) What is it called when strong winds cause a storm of blowing sand? These storms are often in the desert.

8) Where do young adults sometimes go at nights to dance or drink alcohol?

9) What are the white lines in the sky during a big storm called?

What is the mystery word?

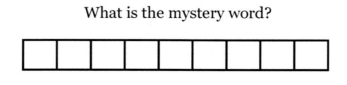

Mystery Word (Ten Letter Words)

Read the clues, write the answers and find the mystery word.

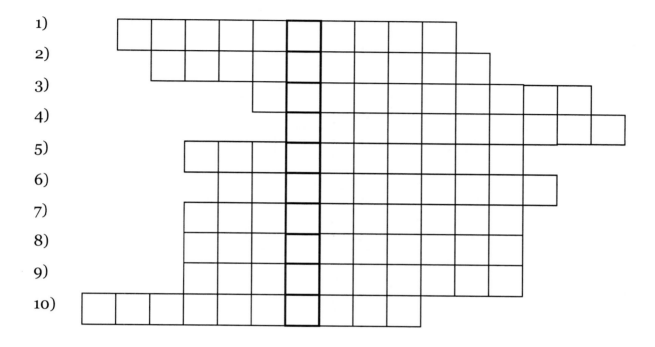

1) What is it called when the earth suddenly starts to shake a lot?

2) What special event do people attend when they finish university?

3) Which sport is similar to boxing but also uses kicking as well as punching?

4) Who works in a zoo and takes care of the animals?   (Plural)

5) Which school do children attend after kindergarten and before middle school?

6) What do we call the player who can use his or her hands in a soccer match?

7) What do we call someone who reads the news on the television?

8) What do people take with a camera?

9) What is the name of the chair that disabled people sometimes have to sit in?

10) What do people put toothpaste on?

What is the mystery word?

Mystery Word (Eleven Letter Words)

Read the clues, write the answers and find the mystery word.

1)
2)
3)
4)
5)
6)
7)
8)
9)
10)
11)

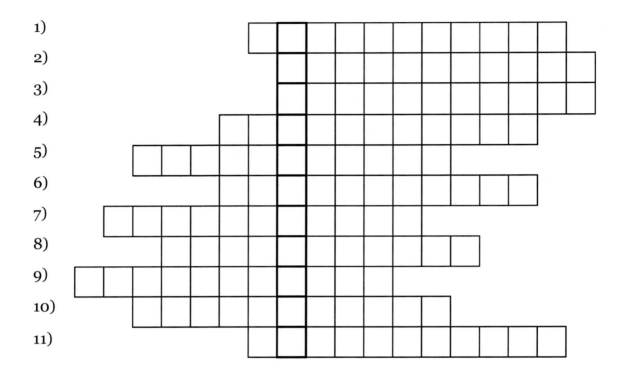

1) What is the art of taking photographs called?

2) What word is an opposite of boring?

3) What is a type of trip where people carry very big bags on their backs?

4) What is a person who walks in his or her sleep called?

5) Which is a rural area sometimes called? (A longer word than country)

6) What are the black finger lines used by police to catch criminals called?

7) What do we call a very large shop that sells food and many other things?

8) What kind of power do computers, televisions and lights need?

9) What is it called when people ski on water?

10) What is a person with one million pounds or dollars called?

11) What do we call knowledge or news in books, newspapers or on the internet?

What is the mystery word?

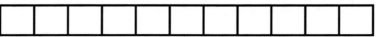

8

Odd One Out

Odd One Out

Read the four choices for each question, think about which word does not belong with the others and why, circle the odd one out and then write a reason for each choice.   After answering the five questions students should make a question of their own to ask orally to their friends.   Use these exercises to practice the students' reading and writing at first.   Then discuss the questions and various answers as a class to develop speaking and listening skills.

Many of the questions have been deliberately created to have more than one possible answer.   For example, the given answer for question one of Odd One Out 1 (see page 97) is June because it has thirty days whereas the other months have thirty-one days.   However, some students will choose January because the other months are in the summer or have good weather.   Some students may even suggest August as it is the only month that does not begin with a 'J'.   The given answer for question two on the same page is carrot because all of the other answers (cabbage, cucumber and alien) are green.   Obviously the answer can just as easily be alien because the remaining choices are vegetables.   Accept all student answers that are logical and well explained. Before doing an Odd One Out activity with a class of students for the first time, be sure to explain and demonstrate the possibility for multiple answers. When students make their own questions it is probably better to encourage them to avoid questions which are a fairly random selection of largely unconnected words that focus simply on answers having or not having a particular letter of the alphabet.

Odd One Out works very well as a non-competitive activity, just focusing on giving as many students as possible, as many chances as possible to participate and try to answer a wide range of questions.   For teachers who want to turn it into more of a game, the recommended method is to allocate two points for matching the given answer in the book and one point for all other possible, logical and well explained answers.

Odd One Out (1)

Read the words, circle the odd one out and then write a reason.

January	June	July	August

cucumber	cabbage	carrot	alien

broken arm	broken heart	broken nose	broken leg

France	Sweden	Germany	Brazil

eyes	arms	nose	ears

Make your own question.   Do not show the answer to your friends.

Odd One Out (2)

Read the words, circle the odd one out and then write a reason.

one	twenty-five	nine	eight

bird	cat	dog	hamster

tennis ball	snowball	football	baseball

bogey	tongue	teeth	gum

recorder	drum	trumpet	flute

Make your own question.   Do not show the answer to your friends.

Odd One Out (3)

Read the words, circle the odd one out and then write a reason.

glasses	false teeth	hearing aid	walking stick

pink	orange	yellow	green

sushi	pasta	spaghetti	pizza

Monday	Wednesday	Friday	Sunday

William	Harry	Jessica	Charles

Make your own question.   Do not show the answer to your friends.

Odd One Out (4)

Read the words, circle the odd one out and then write a reason.

hippo	bat	owl	firefly

mittens	scarf	gloves	wedding ring

curly	bald	straight	wavy

hail	sun	rain	snow

thirty-six	four	eleven	sixteen

Make your own question.   Do not show the answer to your friends.

Odd One Out (5)

Read the words, circle the odd one out and then write a reason.

swan	hen	rooster	chicken

shoes	socks	hiking boots	slippers

cook	doctor	nurse	firefighter

red	yellow	green	black

newspaper	television	internet	microwave

Make your own question.   Do not show the answer to your friends.

Odd One Out (6)

Read the words, circle the odd one out and then write a reason.

scooter	car	motorbike	bicycle

rice	cream	chocolate ice cream	snow

belly button	Adam's apple	toe nails	nostrils

Annie	Jane	James	Julie

London	Paris	Osaka	Washington D.C.

Make your own question.   Do not show the answer to your friends.

Odd One Out (7)

Read the words, circle the odd one out and then write a reason.

butterfly	eagle	whale	magpie

February 14th	September 29th	October 31st	December 25th

wig	sunglasses	cap	hat

sheep	mice	deer	dogs

vitamins	chicken pox	influenza	cough

Make your own question.   Do not show the answer to your friends.

Odd One Out (8)

Read the words, circle the odd one out and then write a reason.

Mars	Jupiter	Saturn	Pluto

steak	pizza	hamburger	sandwich

oven	microwave	refrigerator	campfire

beer	wine	lemonade	whisky

motorbike	unicycle	bicycle	tricycle

Make your own question.   Do not show the answer to your friends.

Odd One Out (9)

Read the words, circle the odd one out and then write a reason.

contact lens	goggles	eyepatch	glasses

cube	square	triangle	circle

kettle	refrigerator	microwave	cooker

June	September	October	November

candle	lamp	mirror	sun

Make your own question.   Do not show the answer to your friends.

Odd One Out (10)

Read the words, circle the odd one out and then write a reason.

electric guitar	acoustic guitar	trombone	violin

mosquito	moth	wasp	owl

legs	knees	toes	heart

nest	feathers	wings	horns

tick tock	quickly	bang	woof

Make your own question.   Do not show the answer to your friends.

9

A-Z Challenges

A-Z Challenges

Students look at the sentence structure and examples, and use the provided information to make a complete set of answers, giving one answer for each pair. Where a letter pair is particularly challenging, additional letters have been grouped together to help the students. Use these exercises to consolidate students' vocabulary, grammar and sentence construction skills.

There is a lot of flexibility as to how the students can complete these tasks. Pairs or small groups work well, with either just one sheet for the group or one sheet per student with all students being required to write every answer. In the case of just giving one sheet to a group, ensure that all students write some sentences perhaps completing alternative answers. Giving students colour pens to clearly distinguish each student's work is often a good idea. The advantage of asking each student to complete a sheet either as part of a pair or team, or as an individual task, is that it allows the teacher to assess more thoroughly, whether the students are constructing grammatically accurate sentences. However, by working in pairs, students can think of vocabulary together and, in classes not grouped by ability, the higher level students can help less able partners.

A-Z Challenges can be used as competitive activities, with the first students to finish winning, continuing through to second and third places and possibly beyond, or as regular class activities. In the latter, continue for a set period of time as allowed for in lesson planning or until most students have finished all or the majority of the letters. Encourage earlier finishers to continue and write more answers on the back of their sheet. They could attempt to complete as much as possible of a second set of answers i.e. one answer on the front and one answer on the back for each letter pair. Alternatively, challenge them to think of answers for the letter within each word pairs that they did not give an answer for the first time. Who can get an answer for the most letters?

A-Z Challenge (Jobs)

Look at the letters and the subject in brackets, think of a job for either letter and write a sentence.   Write one sentence for each letter pair.

_____ want(s) to be a/an _____.

Example One: **cd** (she) - She wants to be a **d**ancer.

Example Two: **op** (I) – I want to be a **p**hotographer.

ab (he):

cd (she):

ef (they):

gh (I):

ij (we):

kl (Jack):

mn (Sophie):

op (I):

qr (she):

st (he):

uv (my friend):

wx (Ruby):

yz (Charles):

A-Z Challenge (Countries)

Look at the letters and the subject in brackets, think of a country and write a sentence.   Write one sentence for each letter pair.

_____ want(s) to go to _____.

Example One: **ab** (I) – I want to go to **Austria**.

Example Two: **ef** (she) – She wants to go to **Egypt**.

ab (I):

cd (he):

ef (she):

gh (I):

ij (they):

kl (William):

mn (Jenny):

op (my grandma):

qr (my brother):

st (she):

uvw (he):

xyz (They):

A-Z Challenge (Zoo Animals)

Look at the letters and try to think of a zoo animal for one of the letters.   Then look at the subject and write a complete sentence.   Write one sentence for each letter pair.

_____ saw a/an _____ at the zoo.

Example One: **ab** (I)   -   I saw a **b**ird at the zoo.

Example Two: **gh** (They) – They saw a **g**orilla at the zoo.

ab (I):

cd (He):

ef (She):

gh (They):

ijk (My friend):

lm (We):

nop (I):

qr (He):

st (She):

uvw (They):

xyz (David):

A-Z Challenge (Food and Drink)

Look at the letters and the subject in brackets, think of a food or drink for either letter and write a sentence.   Write one sentence for each letter pair.

_____ like(s) _____.

Example One: **cd** (she) - She likes **c**arrots.

Example Two: **op** (I) – I like **p**otatoes.

ab (I):

cd (she):

ef (he):

gh (they):

ij (we):

kl (my brother):

mn (my sister):

op (I):

qr (he):

st (she):

uv (my friend):

wx (Mark Bednall):

yz (George):

A-Z Challenge (Adjectives)

Look at the letters and the subject in brackets, think of an adjective for either letter and write a sentence.   Write one sentence for each letter pair.

_____ is/are/am _____.

Example One: **ab** (she) - She is **b**rave.

Example Two: **st** (you) - You are **s**hort.

ab (she):

cd (he):

ef (they):

gh (I):

ij (we):

kl (Mr Jones):

mn (we):

op (I):

qr (they):

st (you):

uv (she):

wx (he):

yz (Harry):

A-Z Challenge (Suggestions)

Look at the letters and think of suggestions.

Write one sentence for each letter pair.

Let's _____.

Example One: **ab** – Let's **b**ake a cake.

Example Two: **gh** – Let's **g**o skating.

ab:

cd:

ef:

gh:

ij:

kl:

mn:

op:

qr:

st:

uv:

wx:

yz:

A-Z Challenge (Exclamations)

Look at the letters and think of exclamations.

Write one sentence for each letter pair.

What (a/an) _____!

Example One: **ab** – What a **b**eautiful rose!

Example Two: **ef** – What an **e**xcellent test score!

ab:

cd:

ef:

gh:

ij:

kl:

mn:

op:

qr:

st:

uv:

wx:

yz:

A-Z Challenge (Past Simple)

Look at the letters, the subject and the time in brackets and then use past simple tense to make a sentence.   Write one sentence for each letter pair.

I/He/She/They _____ yesterday/last night/last week.

Example One: **cd** (he, at breakfast time) - He **c**ooked at breakfast time.

Example Two: **qr** (she, last month) – She **r**etired last month.

ab (I, before sleeping yesterday):

cd (he, at breakfast time):

ef (she, last weekend):

gh (they, last week):

ij (we, two days ago):

kl (Tom, last Wednesday):

mn (he, yesterday):

op (I, at lunchtime):

qr (she, last month):

st (you, last night):

uv (they, last year):

wx (we, 2008):

yz (Jessica, a few minutes ago):

A-Z Challenge (Present Continuous)

Look at the letters and the subject in brackets, think of a future action and write a sentence.   Write one sentence for each letter pair.

_____ am/is/are   _____ing _____.

Example One: **st** (Mr Brown) – Mr Brown is **t**eaching English.

Example Two: **yz** (he) – He is **z**igzagging in the road.

ab (they):

cd (he):

ef (she):

gh (I):

ij (Joe):

kl (my mother):

mn (Robert):

op (Kate):

qr (she):

st (Mr Brown):

uv (we):

wx (I):

yz (he):

A-Z Challenge (Future Actions)

Look at the letters and the subject in brackets, think of a future action and write a sentence.   Write one sentence for each letter pair.

_____ going to _____.

Example One: **cd** (she) – She's going to **si**t down over there.

Example Two: **yz** (Lucy) – Lucy's going to **zi**p her jacket up.

ab (he):

cd (she):

ef (they):

gh (I):

ij (we):

kl (John Smith):

mn (my friend):

op (he):

qr (she):

st (they):

uv (I):

wx (We):

yz (Lucy):

10

Apple-Elephant Quizzes

Apple-Elephant Quizzes

Students read the questions, look at the letters they have as hints and use them to solve the clues. Use the quizzes in this section to practise the students' reading, understanding and vocabulary.

Before starting a game, make sure that the students understand the topic. For instance, if they are doing the 'Uncountable Nouns' quiz, ensure they understand the concept giving examples if necessary. If they are doing the 'Square and Rectangular Objects' or 'Circular and Round Objects' quizzes, draw a simple illustration on the board and give relevant examples. When the game begins, the students look at the starter word at the top of the page and read the first question. The students must then write the answer under the question using the last letter of the previous answer as the first letter of the new answer and continue in the same way for each question down to the bottom of the page where the last question and answer are given. Answers should be given in the singular form unless otherwise stated on the sheet. *

Before playing the game for the first time, point out to the students that if they get stuck on a question, they can also try to answer in reverse, going to the bottom and using the first letter of the previous answer as the last letter of a new question and try and meet their answers in the middle, finally having the first and last letter to help them with their final question. Students could also try and answer a question from somewhere in the middle without any first or last letters as a hint although if they do that and answer incorrectly, they risk the majority of their quiz paper being wrong.

This activity works very well in pairs, although students could also work in slightly bigger groups. Continue until one pair or team has all the right answers, and then go through the answers as a class. In a large class, the teacher could allow play to continue until three teams have finished (first, second and third places).

---

* In the Animal Quiz (see page 121), students may find the question about Santa very difficult. Consider using YouTube to play Rudolph the Red Nosed Reindeer as a hint during the game.

<u>Apple – Elephant Quiz (Animals)</u>

zebra

Which animal is very similar to a crocodile?

Which animal helps Santa deliver presents?

Which animal is usually dark in color and looks similar to a mouse but is a little bit bigger?

Which animal is a large cat, has stripes and is usually seen in Asia?

Which animal is a popular pet with big ears?

Which animal lives in or near water, has a shell and can sometimes live to more than one hundred years old?

Which animal starts and finishes with the same letter?

Which animal is the largest land animal?

Which big bird is often eaten at Christmas?   It is also the name of a country.

turkey

Apple – Elephant Quiz (Going on a Trip)

watch

↓

What do people often wear on their heads?

What do people need to buy before taking their families on a bus or train? (Plural)

What very long things do some people take on a skiing trip?

What do people wear over their eyes if they go on a trip to a very sunny place?

What do people use with water when they wash their hands?

What very important small book do you have to take if you are going on a trip to another country?

What do people usually sleep inside on a camping trip?

What is usually used to dry a person's body after taking a shower?

Where do people often put their lunch before going on a trip or picnic?

↓

lunch box

Apple – Elephant Quiz (Square and Rectangular Objects)

bus

↓

What small thing do many people buy at the post office before sending a letter?

What is the name of the very important small book people need when they visit another country?

What do people usually buy before entering an amusement park, zoo or museum?

What do students or teachers look at when they want to know their next class?

What do people often use when they want to change something written in pencil?

What do people use to change the channel on a TV without standing up?

What do people write or print on paper and then send at the post office?

What is the name of a four sided shape with two sides longer than the other two?

What do people put a letter inside before sending it?

envelope

Apple – Elephant Quiz (Circular and Round Objects)

U.F.O.

↓

Which vegetable sometimes makes people cry when they cut or slice it?

What do some women wear around their necks?
(Plural)

What do people use with water to wash their faces?

What do people often put food on after cooking and before eating?

Which planet do we live on?

Which body part is the brain inside?

Which musical instrument has a circular top, is played with a stick or by hand, and is an important instrument in many bands?

Which fruit is round, big and yellow?

Which fruit is also the name of a colour?

↓

orange

<u>Apple – Elephant Quiz (Uncountable Nouns)</u>

meat

Which hot drink is very popular instead of coffee?

What is outside, sometimes hot and sometimes cold, and cannot be seen?

What is it called when drops of water fall from the sky?

Which food is very long and often eaten with chopsticks?

What is white and sometimes put on food?   It can also be found in the sea.

What do American people call things that they throw away?
The British word for it is rubbish.

What do most people have on the top of their heads?

Which food is white and very popular in Asia?

What kind of power is used for many lights and machines?

electricity

Apple – Elephant Quiz (Countable Nouns)

book

What do children play with outside, especially on a windy day?

What is the name of the body part in the middle of the arm?

What is found in most rooms of buildings and can be opened or closed?

What do birds and planes have that help them to fly?   (Singular)

What is an outdoor place where people can play, eat food or see flowers?
Many houses have one or two.

Who cares for sick people and helps doctors or dentists?

What is the name of a person, who designs, makes or repairs engines?

What is the name of a romantic red flower?

What is a person who someone really hates called?

enemy

Apple – Elephant Quiz (Body Parts - Easy)

arm

What do people open to eat?

Which body part do people wash the most?
(Plural)

What do people have all over their bodies?

What is between the head and shoulders?

What is about half way down a leg?

What do people use to see?

Which body part do we use to hear sounds?
(Plural)

What is at the top of an arm?

Where is a wedding ring worn?

ring finger

Apple – Elephant Quiz (Body Parts - Difficult)

collarbone

↓

What do people use to hear?

Humans have twenty-four of these.   They are curved bones.   What are they?
(Write the singular)

What do people use to think?

What is another name for the belly button?

Which body organ helps people breath?

What is in the mouth and joined to the teeth?
It is also the name of something people chew.

Which body part helps to show strength, especially in the arms?

Which body part is in the ear and sounds like a musical instrument?

What is a small dark brown spot on the skin called?

↓

mole

Apple – Elephant Quiz (Light Objects)

leaf

↓

What do birds have many of?

What is often used for wrapping Christmas and birthday presents?

What is small, usually white and often seen on a dinner table?
It is used for cleaning the hands and face, and to stop food going on a person.

Which small healthy food do squirrels like to eat?

Other than water, what do you put in a cup when you want to make a cup of tea?
(Two words)

Which food is small, looks a little bit like an onion, has a strong smell and taste, and often gives a person bad breath?

Which unhealthy thing do many people smoke in their mouths?

What is usually small and worn in an ear?

What is the name of a small animal, often kept as a pet?

↓

guinea pig

<u>Apple – Elephant Quiz (Heavy Objects)</u>

encyclopedia

↓

What is the name of a glass tank used for keeping fish?

What is used to cook food very quickly, including cooked food that has gone cold?

What is the name of a bicycle often used inside to exercise?
(Two words)

What is the name of a very big animal with large ears?

What do people like to watch at home?
It has a long name and a very short name.   Use the short one.

Which electrical appliance is often used for cleaning up dirt and dust?
(Two words)

What machine can be big or small and often looks like a human?

Which object with springs do people often jump up and down on?
It can often be seen in a gymnasium.

What gives power to cars or trains to help them move?

↓

engine

Answers

A-Z Quiz One (Page 13)

apple, ball, cat, dice, egg, fish, go, hello, ice cream, jelly, king, love, monkey, nine, octopus, piano, quiet, raining, Saturday, tree, U.F.O., violin (also accept viola), watermelon, x-ray, zoo

A-Z Quiz Two (Page 14)

airplane, breakfast, chair, die, English, fourteen, giraffe, happy, ice skate (also accept ice hockey as a right answer), jam, kangaroo, leg, menu, no, orange, ping pong, queen, rainbow, school, television, umbrella, vase, winter, yellow, zero

A-Z Quiz Three (Page 15)

alligator, bike/bicycle, Christmas, dentist, eighteen, fat, grandpa/grandfather, hot, in, jeans, kick, library, moon, nose, old, present, quiz, rabbit, ship, talk, up, vegetable, watch, yesterday, zebra

A-Z Quiz Four (Page 16)

afternoon, baseball, caterpillar, dinosaur, early, fur, glass, handsome, interview, jump, key, lemon, magician, never, open, P.E./physical education, quack, road, September, turkey, uncle, vet, war, yo-yo, zookeeper

A-Z Quiz Five (Page 17)

Argentina, biscuits, crawl, dictionary, eagle, fan, grass, half, island, joke, kite, lady, movie, naughty, office, pilot, quarter, robot, sunburn, tick tock, unicorn, Valentine's Day, wish, yoghurt, zone

A-Z Quiz Six (Page 18)

allergy, bought, cushion, diary, enter, forest, ghosts, Halloween, Italy, jazz, kitchen, leaves, Mars, nuts, October, penguin, quickly, radio, soap, tarantula, under, vote, weak, yard, zoom in

A-Z Quiz Seven (Page 19)

address, bakery, customer, dig, exam, France, geography, hill, internet, jigsaw, kiss, late, mouse, nap, owl, plate, quicksand, roof, shampoo, trophy, uniform, vanilla, why, year, zip

A-Z Quiz Eight (Page 20)

aliens, blueberry, chef, directions, elbow, factory, (The) Great Wall of China, hole, Italy, January, kids, lego, million, newspaper, ox, parrot, qwerty, remote control, sundae, timetable, unlucky, veins, wig, yawn, Zimbabwe

A-Z Quiz Nine (Page 21)

ankle, balloon, camel, duet, eye-brow, favourite, gold, hide and seek, inch, jungle, kitten, lid, Mercury, needle, onion, palace, quill, return, sister-in-law, telescope, university, volcano, wings, xylophone, Zeus

A-Z Quiz Ten (Page 22)

angel, beard, clockwise, disabled, exercise, full moon, genius, hero, India, jogging, knife, lamb, mirror, New Year's Day, opera, pirate, Qatar, ring, swallow, tusks, u-turn, volleyball, whisper, yucky, zit

Categories Game (Pages 23 to 34)
Answers will vary.   Check the answers as a class.   The teacher adjudicates where necessary.

5, 4, 3, 2, 1 Game (Answer order: top left, top right, middle left, middle right, bottom left, bottom right)

5, 4, 3, 2, 1 Jobs Game (Page 37): teacher, farmer, president (also accept prime minister), train driver, scientist, author/writer

5, 4, 3, 2, 1 Food Game (Page 38): rice, carrot, spaghetti, cake, cereal, strawberry

5, 4, 3, 2, 1 Musical Instruments (Page 39): triangle, drum, tambourine, piano, keyboard, recorder

5, 4, 3, 2, 1 Places (Page 40): airport, post office, soccer stadium, farm, coffee shop, swimming pool

5, 4, 3, 2, 1 Animals Game (Page 41): crocodile, rabbit, elephant, mouse, horse, snake

5, 4, 3, 2, 1 Sports Game (Page 42): baseball, swimming, golf, table tennis/ping pong, ice hockey, boxing

5, 4, 3, 2, 1 Household Objects (Page 43): shower, computer, microwave, bed, cups, toothbrush

5, 4, 3, 2, 1 In the Supermarket (Page 44): milk, gum, toilet paper, water, shopping trolley/shopping cart, car park/parking lot

5, 4, 3, 2, 1 Countries (Page 45): China, Brazil, Finland, Netherlands/Holland, France, Italy

5, 4, 3, 2, 1 Clothing and Accessories (Page 46): scarf, earring, school uniform, suit, ring, socks

Anagrams (Answer order: From top to bottom)

Anagrams 1: Days of the Week (Page 49): Monday, Tuesday, Wednesday, Thursday, Friday, Saturday, Sunday, today, yesterday, tomorrow

Anagrams 2: Months (Page 50): June (6), May (5), July (7), April (4), March (3), August (8), October (10), December (12), September (9), January (1), November (11), February (2)

Anagrams 3: Feelings and Emotions (Page 51): happy, sad, angry, tired, sick, bored, scared, excited, worried, surprised

Anagrams 4: Drinks (Page 52): tea, milk, cola, wine, beer, water, coffee, lemonade, milkshake, orange juice

Anagrams 5: Vegetables (Page 53): pea, corn, onion, carrot, pepper, potato, cabbage, pumpkin, cucumber, mushroom

Anagrams 6: Hobbies (Page 54): bowling, playing tennis, painting, playing the piano, playing badminton, swimming, playing basketball, cooking, playing computer games, skateboarding

Anagrams 7: Dangerous and Scary Activities (Page 55): skiing, jet skiing, bungee jump, parachute jump, scuba diving, bullfighting, rock climbing, snowboarding, rollercoaster, canoeing

Anagrams 8: Space (Page 56): U.F.O., Jupiter, Mars, Earth, Saturn, Mercury, Venus, Neptune, Uranus, The Moon

Anagrams 9: Forms of Transport A (Page 57): car, bus, van, boat, taxi, lorry, train, truck, subway, bicycle

Anagrams 10: Forms of Transport B (Page 58): canoe, scooter, police car, fire engine, helicopter, motorbike, tractor, ambulance, unicycle, double decker bus

Wordsearch 1: Natural Disasters (Page 61)
Horizontal: earthquake, drought, famine, blizzard, cyclone
Vertical: avalanche, flood, tsunami, hurricane
Diagonal: tornado

Wordsearch 2: World Cities (Page 62)
Horizontal: London, Seoul, Sydney, Budapest
Vertical: Beijing
Diagonal: Rome, Paris, Tokyo

Wordsearch 3: Soccer World Cup Winners (Page 63)
Horizontal: Uruguay, England, Spain, Argentina, Brazil
Vertical: Italy, Germany, France

Wordsearch 4: Famous Monuments (Page 64)
Answers from top to bottom: Greece, Australia, England, Italy, France, China, Canada, Egypt, America, India
Horizontal: Greece, Australia, England, Italy, France, India
Vertical: Canada, Egypt, America
Diagonal: China

Wordsearch 5: Nationalities (Page 65)
Answers from top to bottom: American, Canadian, Chinese, English, French, Italian, Japanese, Swiss
Horizontal: American, Chinese, English, French, Italy, Japanese
Vertical: Swiss
Diagonal: Canadian

Wordsearch 6: Animal Sounds (Page 66)

Answers from top to bottom: sheep, bird, chicken, cat, horse, pig, duck, frog, mouse, dog

Horizontal: baa, cluck, miaow, neigh, quack, ribbit, squeak

Vertical: chirp, oink

Diagonal: woof

Wordsearch 7: Opposites (Page 67)

Answers from top to bottom: short, messy, thin, outside, young, lazy, safe, light

Horizontal: short, thin

Vertical: messy, outside, safe, light

Diagonal: young, lazy

Wordsearch 8: Weather (Page 68)

Horizontal: lightning, sunny, rainy, foggy, windy, snowy, hot

Vertical: cold, icy, cloudy

(The teacher checks the students' drawings.)

Wordsearch 9: Irregular Verbs (Page 69)

Answers from top to bottom: bought, came, drank, felt, flew, went, paid, taught

Horizontal: bought, came

Vertical: drank, went, paid

Diagonal: felt, flew, taught

(The teacher checks the students' use of the irregular verbs in sentences.)

Wordsearch 10: Homophones (Page 70)

Answers from top to bottom: sun, eight, sea, night, witch, deer, bear, flower

Horizontal: sun, sea, witch, bear

Vertical: eight, deer

Diagonal: night, flower

(The teacher checks the students' drawings and illustrations.)

Crosswords

Before School (Page 73)

Across: 1) up   4) uniform   5) breakfast   7) shower   8) wash   9) get

Down: 2) put   3) drink   6) teeth   8) wake

After School (Page 74)

Across: 2) get   3) read   6) friends   7) homework   8) listen

Down: 1) dishes   2) games   4) dinner   5) watch   6) family

Before Sleeping (Page 75)

Across: 1) book   2) put   3) wash   6) eat   7) off   8) close

Down: 1) brush   3) write   4) school   5) lie

At the Weekend (Page 76)

Across: 1) go   3) television   5) exercise   6) watch   8) shopping

Down: 1) get   2) trip   4) visit   7) homework   9) play

Life of a Baby (Page 77)

Across: 2) crawl   5) hospital   6) talking   9) diaper

Down: 1) fall   2) cry   3) walking   4) sleep   7) nap   8) drink

Numbers (Page 78)

Across: 1) twenty-six   2) four   4) twenty-four   8) eleven

Down: 1) thirty-one   3) zero   4) two   5) eight   6) three   7) ten

Words Without Vowels (Page 79)

Across: 2) sky   3) dry   5) try   8) rhythm   9) why

Down: 1) cry   2) shy   4) rhythms   6) fry   7) gym

Phrasal Verbs 1 (Page 80)

Across: 2) grow   5) turn   7) hurry   8) call   9) wash

Down: 1) go   3) watch   4) knock   5) try   6) blow

Phrasal Verbs 2 (Page 81)

Across: 1) stand   2) get   3) take   4) dress   7) throw

Down: 1) shut   2) give   3) turn   5) switch   6) zoom

Phrasal Verbs 3 (Page 82)

Across: 2) look   3) come   6) away   7) break   8) find

Down: 1) move   3) close   4) wake   5) save   7) burn

Mystery Word (Answer order: from top to bottom plus the mystery word in bold)

Mystery Word: In the Bathroom (Page 85)

towel, soap, toilet paper, toilet, shampoo, brush, shower, bathtub, sink, toothpaste, **toothbrush**

Mystery Word: In the Kitchen (Page 86)

cooker, dishes, bowl, spoon, saucer, plate, knife, microwave, fork, sink, **chopsticks**

Mystery Word: In the Bedroom (Page 87)

computer, quilt, pillow, bed, toys, lamp, mirror, desk, pajamas/pyjamas, **cupboards**

Mystery Word: In the Living Room (Page 88)

table, vase, light, bookcase, plant, chair, sofa, fan, stereo, **telephone**

Mystery Word: Words with the letter X (Page 89)

x-ray, oxygen, example, fox, expensive, exchange, boxing, next, sixteen, **xylophone**

Mystery Word: Fruit (Page 90)

kiwi, apple, strawberry, pineapple, grapes, lemon, orange, blueberry, mango, banana, **watermelon**

Mystery Word: On the Beach (Page 91)

sea, sunglasses, sand, drink, crab, surfboard, frisbee, towel, shell, beach ball, **sandcastle**

Mystery Word: Nine Letter Words (Page 92)

bookstore, countdown, chocolate, sometimes, excellent, president, sandstorm, nightclub, lightning, **boomerang**

Mystery Word: Ten Letter Words (Page 93)

earthquake, graduation, kickboxing, zookeepers, elementary, goalkeeper, newsreader, photograph, wheelchair, toothbrush, **quizmaster**

Mystery Word: Eleven Letter Words (Page 94)

photography, interesting, backpacking, sleepwalker, countryside, fingerprint, supermarket, electricity, waterskiing, millionaire, **hibernation**

Odd One Out (The following are sample answers.   Some questions have several other possibilities and all logically explained student choices as the odd one out should be given credit.   Answers go from top to bottom.)

Odd One Out 1 (Page 97)

June - The others have thirty-one days.

Carrot - The others are green.

Broken heart - The others are physical injuries.

Brazil – The others are in Europe.

Nose – People normally have two eyes, ears and arms but only one nose.

Odd One Out 2 (Page 98)

Eight – The others are odd numbers.

Bird – The others have four legs.

Snowball – The others are balls used to play sport.

Bogey – The others are found in the mouth.

Drum – The others are wind instruments.

Odd One Out 3 (Page 99)

Walking stick - The others are worn.

Pink – The others are colours of a rainbow.

Sushi – The others are from Italy.

Sunday – The others are school days.

Jessica – The others are boys' names.

Odd One Out 4 (Page 100)

Hippo - The others are nocturnal animals.

Scarf – The others are worn on hands.

Bald – The others are hairstyles.

Sun – The others fall from the sky.

Eleven – The others are even numbers.

Odd One Out 5 (Page 101)

Swan - The others are chickens.

Socks – The others are kinds of footwear rather than clothes.

Firefighter – The others usually wear white clothes or uniform.

Black – The others are traffic light colours.

Microwave – The others are sources of news.

Odd One Out 6 (Page 102)

Car - The others have two wheels.

Chocolate ice cream – The others are white.

Adam's Apple – Only a man has an Adam's apple.   Both males and females have the other body parts.

James – The others are girls' names.

Osaka – The others are capital cities.

Odd One Out 7 (Page 103)

Whale - The others can fly.

September 29th – The others are special days in multiple countries (Valentine's, Halloween and Christmas).

Sunglasses – The others are always worn on the head.

Dogs – The others are already plurals without adding a 's'.

Vitamins – The others are illnesses.

Odd One Out 8 (Page 104)

Pluto - The others are planets (Pluto has been demoted to 'dwarf planet' status).

Steak – The others are commonly held in the hands when eating.

Refrigerator – The others are used for cooking or heating food.

Lemonade – The others are forms of alcohol.

Motorbike – The others are kinds of bicycles.

Odd One Out 9 (Page 105)

Contact lens - The others are worn over the eyes.   Contact lens are worn in the eyes.

Cube – The others are 2D shapes.

Refrigerator – The others are used for making food or drink hotter.

October – The others have thirty days.

Mirror – The others are sources of light.

Odd One Out 10 (Page 106)

Trombone - The others are string instruments.

Owl – The others are insects.

Heart – The others are external body parts.

Horns – The others are all related to birds.

Quickly – The others are sounds.

A-Z Challenges (The following are sample answers.   There are a massive number of alternative possible answers.   The letter in bold highlights which of the letter pair or selection is being used)

Jobs (Page 109): He wants to be an **a**ctor.   She wants to be a **d**octor.   They want to be **f**irefighters.   I want to be a **g**ardener.   We want to be **j**ournalists.   Jack wants to be a **l**awyer.   Sophie wants to be a **n**urse.   I want to be a **p**olice officer.   She wants to be a **r**eporter.   He wants to be a **t**eacher.   My friend wants to be a **v**et.   Ruby wants to be a **w**riter.   Charles wants to be a **z**ookeeper.

Countries (Page 110): I want to go to **B**elgium.   He wants to go to **D**enmark.   She wants to go to **F**inland.   I want to go to **G**reenland.   They want to go to **I**celand.   William wants to go to **L**uxembourg.   Jenny wants to go to **N**orway.   My grandma wants to go to **P**oland.   My brother wants to go to **R**ussia.   She wants to go to **S**witzerland.   He wants to go to **U**ruguay.   They want to go to **Z**ambia.

Zoo Animals (Page 111): I saw a **b**ear at the zoo.   He saw a **d**olphin at the zoo.   She saw an **e**lephant at the zoo.   They saw a **g**iraffe at the zoo.   My friend saw a **k**oala at the zoo.   We saw a **m**onkey at the zoo.   I saw a **p**anda at the zoo.   He saw a **r**abbit at the zoo.   She saw a **t**iger at the zoo.   They saw a **w**olf at the zoo.   David saw a **z**ebra at the zoo.

Food and Drink (Page 112): I like **b**acon.   She likes **c**ake.   He likes **e**ggs.   They like **h**am.   We like **i**ce cream.   My brother likes **l**ettuce.   My sister likes **m**ilkshakes.   I like **p**eas.   He likes **r**aw fish.   She likes **s**ausages.   My friend likes **v**egetable soup.   Mark Bednall likes **w**hisky.   George likes **y**oghurt.

Adjectives (Page 113): She is **b**eautiful.   He is **c**lever.   They are **f**unny.   I am **h**appy.   We are **j**ealous.   Mr Jones is **l**azy.   We are **n**ice.   I am **o**ld.   They are **q**uiet.   You are **t**all.   She is **u**pset.   He is **w**eak.   Harry is **y**oung.

Suggestions (Page 114): Let's **b**uy some stickers.   Let's **d**ance.   Let's **f**inish quickly.   Let's **g**o shopping.   Let's **i**nvite John.   Let's **l**eave early.   Let's **m**ake a card.   Let's **p**lay basketball.   Let's **q**ueue up.   Let's **t**ry one more time.   Let's **u**se the elevator.   Let's **w**atch a movie.   Let's **z**oom in on that bird.

Exclamations (Page 115): What a **b**eautiful flower!   What a **c**ute baby!   What a **f**unny clown!   What a **g**reat idea!   What an **i**cy road!   What a **k**ind old man!   What a **n**ice boy!   What a **p**retty girl!   What a **r**ainy day!   What a **s**urprise!   What an **u**gly looking dog!   What a **w**eird hairstyle!   What a **y**ummy cake!

Past Simple Tense (Page 116): I **b**rushed my teeth before sleeping yesterday.   He **d**rank coffee at breakfast time.   She **e**xercised last weekend.   They **h**ad a fight last week.   We **i**nvited him to our house two days ago.

Tom **l**eft our school last Wednesday.   He **m**et his new manager yesterday.   I **p**layed with my friends at lunchtime.   She **q**uit her job last month.   You **s**tayed up too late last night.   They **v**isited their friend in Chile last year.   We **w**ent to Scotland in 2008.   Jessica **y**awned a few minutes ago.

Present Continuous (Page 117): They are **b**aking a cake.   He is **d**oing his homework.   She is **e**ating dinner. I am **h**elping my mother.   Joe is **j**uggling.   My mother is **k**nitting some clothes.   Robert is **m**aking a plan. Kate is **p**ainting a picture.   She is **r**eading a comic.   Mr Brown is **t**alking on the telephone.   We are **v**isiting our grandmother.   I am **w**alking to school.   He is **z**igzagging in the road.

Future Actions (Page 118): He is going to **b**uy a car.   She is going to **d**esign some new clothes.   They are going to **f**ind part-time jobs.   I am going to **g**o to university.   We are going to **i**gnore him.   John Smith is going to **l**ie down.   My friend is going to **m**emorize the words for the test.   He is going to **p**ick some fruit.   She is going to **r**aise a pet.   They are going to **s**tudy harder in the future.   I am going to **u**pload a photo.   We are going to **w**atch a musical.   Lucy is going to **y**ell at Tony when she sees him.

Apple-Elephant Quizzes (Answer order: From top to bottom)

Animals (Page 121): zebra, alligator, reindeer, rat, tiger, rabbit, turtle, eagle, elephant, turkey

Going on a Trip (Page 122): watch, hot, tickets, skis, sunglasses, soap, passport, tent, towel, lunch box

Square and Rectangular Objects (Page 123): bus, stamp, passport, ticket, timetable, eraser, remote control, letter, rectangle, envelope

Circular and Round Objects (Page 124): U.F.O., onion, necklaces, soap, plate, Earth, head, drum, mango, orange

Uncountable Nouns (Page 125): meat, tea, air, rain, noodles, salt, trash, hair, rice, electricity

Countable Nouns (Page 126): book, kite, elbow, window, wing, garden, nurse, engineer, rose, enemy

Body Parts – Easy (Page 127): arm, mouth, hands, skin, neck, knee, eye, ears, shoulder, ring finger

Body Parts – Difficult (Page 128): collarbone, ear, rib, brain, navel, lung, gum, muscle, eardrum, mole

Light Objects (Page 129): leaf, feather, ribbon, napkin, nut, tea bag, garlic, cigarette, earring, guinea pig

Heavy Objects (Page 130): encyclopedia, aquarium, microwave, exercise bike, elephant, TV, vacuum cleaner, robot, trampoline, engine

Index

About the author

Adrian Bozon is a qualified England primary school teacher. He has also taught English as a foreign language to students of all ages, most notably for several years in a South Korean elementary school. He has taught students of all ability levels in small, medium and large class sizes. He has taught in various teaching environments including extensive experience of team-teaching in addition to regular solo-teaching. Adrian has also worked closely with over two hundred Korean student teachers.

Also by Adrian Bozon

100 Great EFL Games: Exciting Language Games for Young Learners.

ISBN 978-0956796806

Lightning Source UK Ltd.
Milton Keynes UK
UKOW022323010612

193798UK00009B/4/P